My tale begins long ago
on a hillside in a country far away.
It was spring, and I was hanging out
with one of my wooly buddies.

Suddenly a young lad with
a serious pair of sheers
came along and rather rudely
separated me from my wooly
coat.

I thought I would have my
thick coat forever but
it was not to be, as my owners
had big plans for my wool.
Since summer was just ahead,
I really did not need my coat.
But still it was a shocking experience.

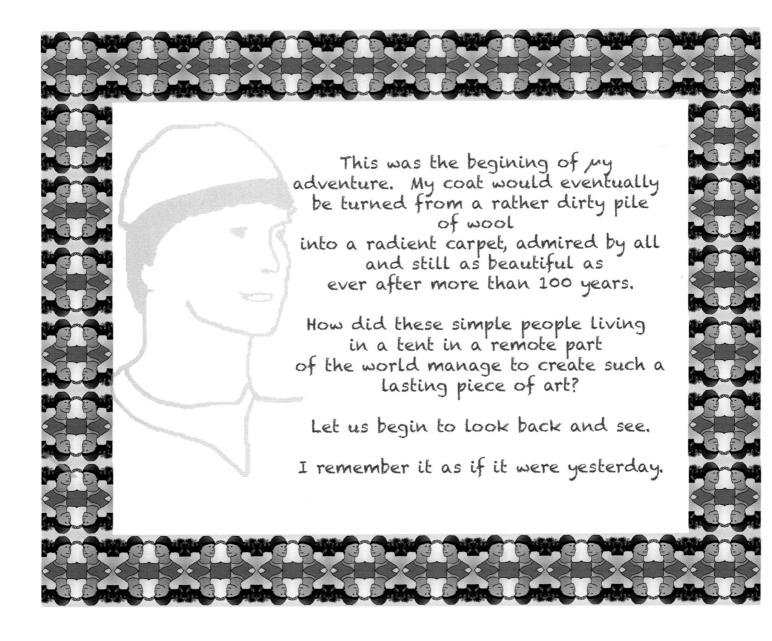

This was the begining of my adventure. My coat would eventually be turned from a rather dirty pile of wool into a radient carpet, admired by all and still as beautiful as ever after more than 100 years.

How did these simple people living in a tent in a remote part of the world manage to create such a lasting piece of art?

Let us begin to look back and see.

I remember it as if it were yesterday.

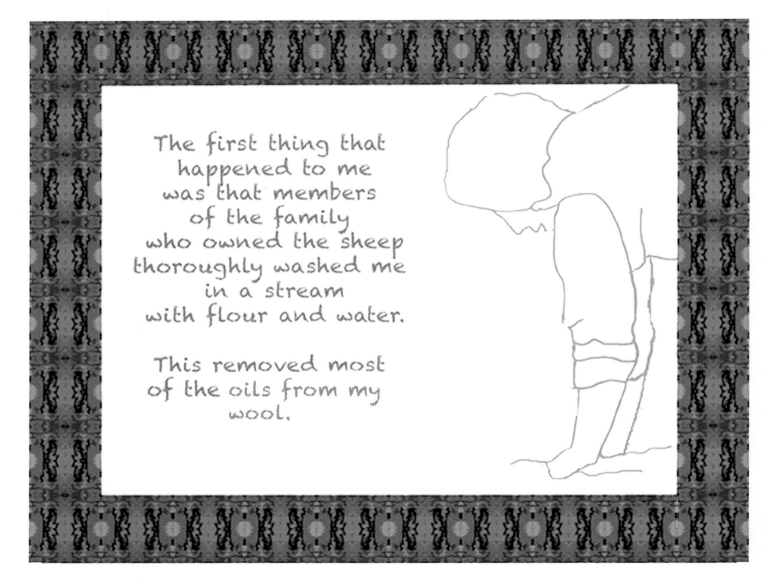

The first thing that
happened to me
was that members
of the family
who owned the sheep
thoroughly washed me
in a stream
with flour and water.

This removed most
of the oils from my
wool.

Then my wool was
laid out to dry
in the sun.

Suddenly.
Out of nowhere more
family members came
along with long sticks
and beat my wool until
it was quite fluffy.

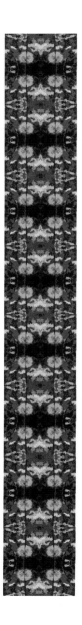

These simple people lived
in a tent very close to nature.
There was a constant pattern to their lives
that helped them cope with the extremes
of temperature and limited food supply.
Their days were filled with
routine tasks and hard work,
but on good days the rhythm of life
filled their mind and love of nature
filled their hearts.

This family had a daughter named
Talya. She needed a gift for her future
husband. I was to be that gift, a beautiful
Turkish rug.

It takes a long time for one
family to weave a rug, so they began
when Talya was just a girl
and she helped in my creation.

Talya loved nature.
She loved the creatures of the field,
the birds and the flowers.
The patterns of some of these loved things
would be included in the rug created
with my wool.

Talya's Mother and sister took my fluffy wool and spun it into yarn.

Meanwhile her father began
to design the pattern for the rug.

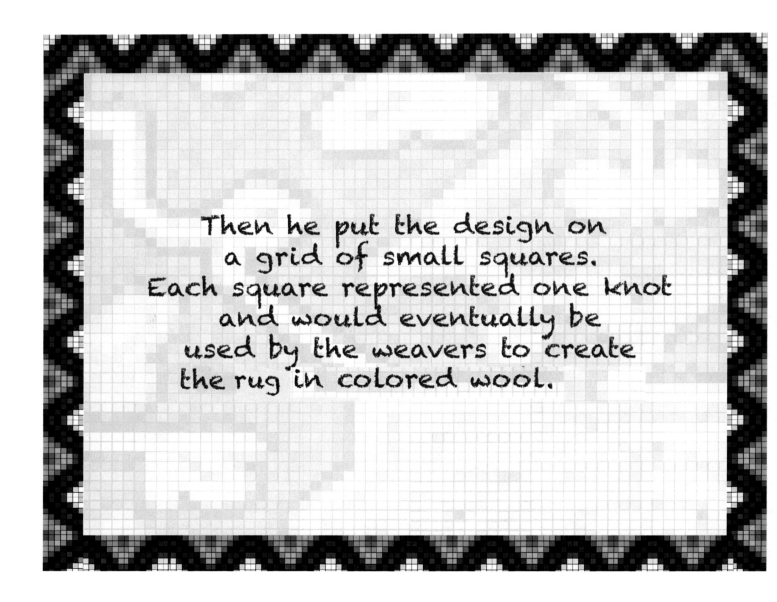

Then he put the design on
a grid of small squares.
Each square represented one knot
and would eventually be
used by the weavers to create
the rug in colored wool.

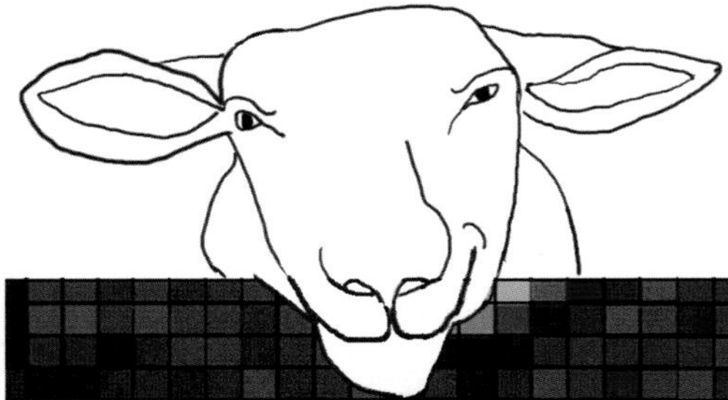

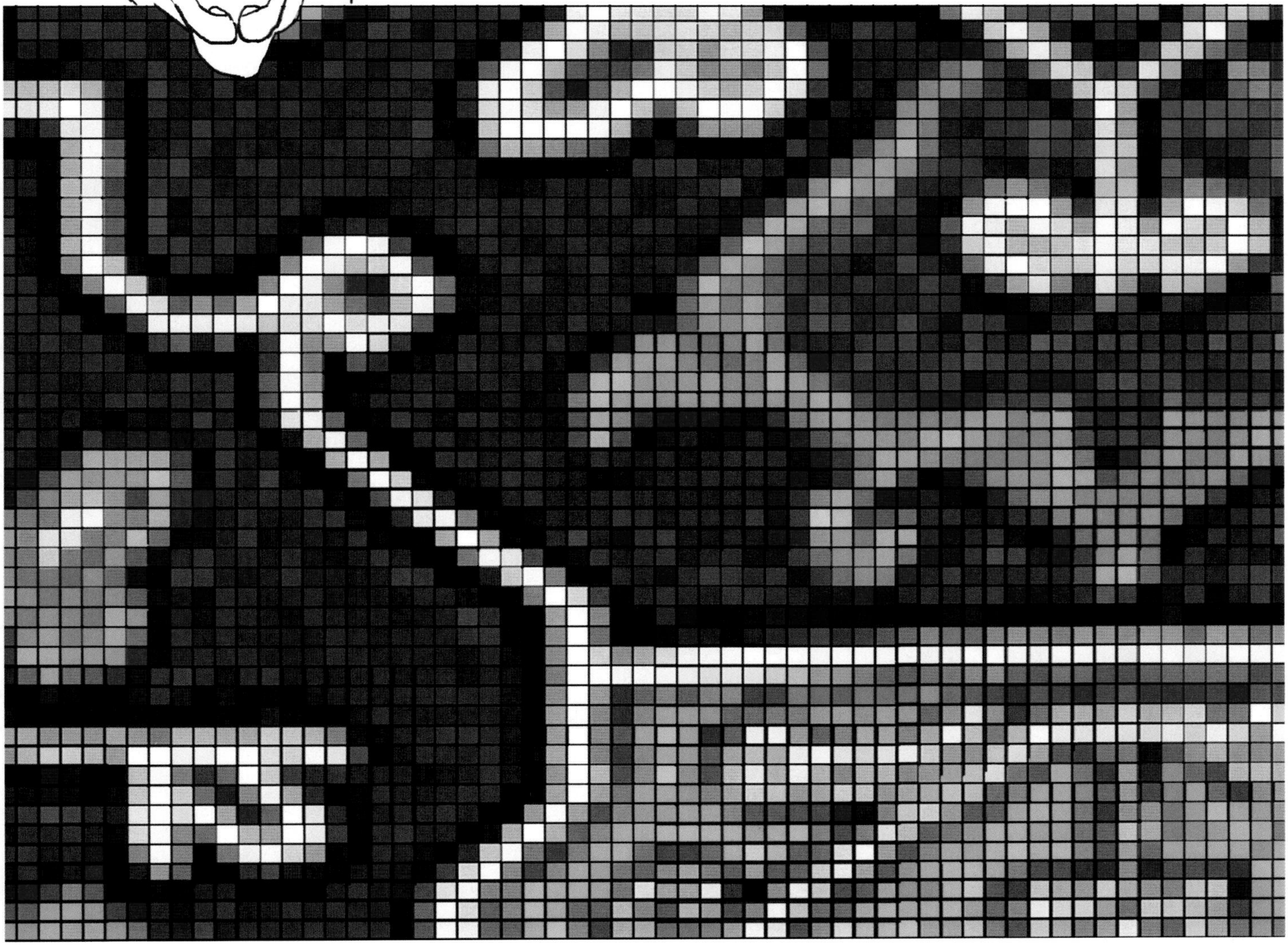

When the cartoon was completed,
Talya's Father and brother
began gathering flowers,
vegetables, and roots to make
the dyes necessary to complete
the rug

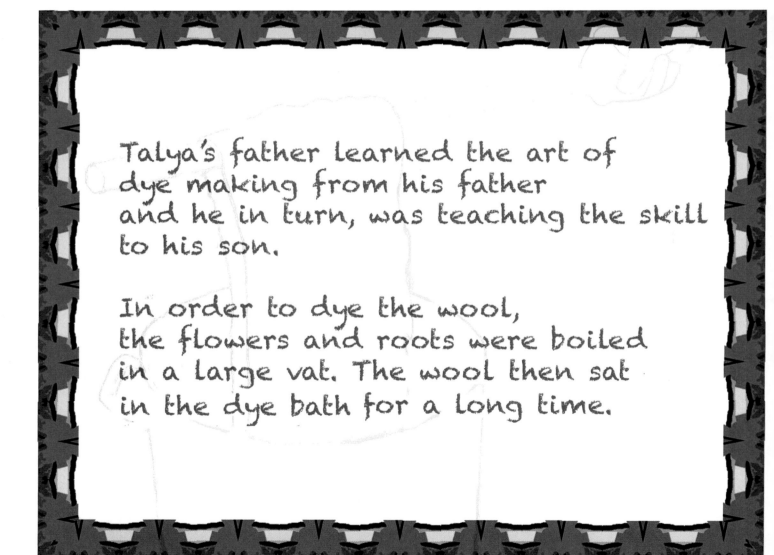

Talya's father learned the art of
dye making from his father
and he in turn, was teaching the skill
to his son.

In order to dye the wool,
the flowers and roots were boiled
in a large vat. The wool then sat
in the dye bath for a long time.

Then it was dried in the sun to set the color. It is impossible to dye enough wool at any one time to complete a whole rug, so the dying is done in batches. Each batch of any one color is slightly different. It is this slight color variation that creates the rich beauty of hand dyed oriental rugs. This color actually becomes more mellow as it ages.

Now it was time for Talya's mother
to get ready to weave.

Talya watched, holding her
pet bird, as her mother put my thread
on the loom by wrapping it around
from top to bottom. This vertical wrap is
called the warp.

Her mother put a pole called
a heddle under every other thread.

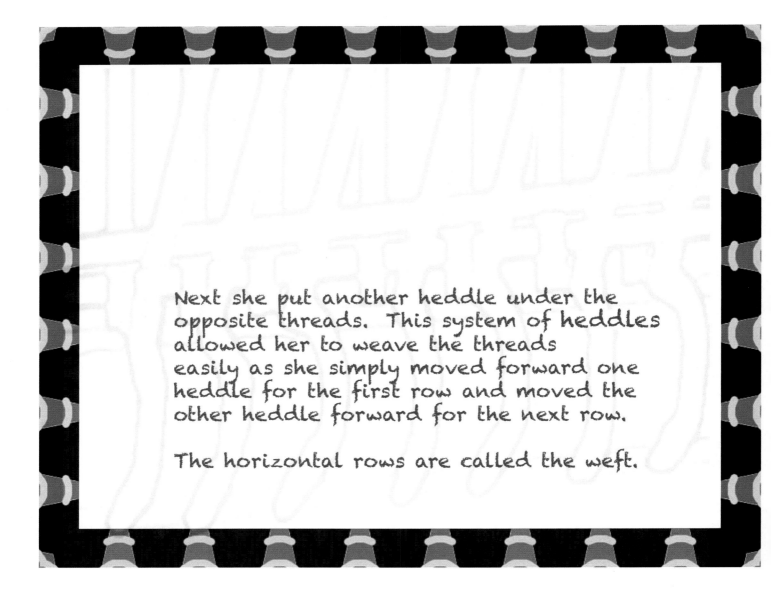

Next she put another heddle under the opposite threads. This system of heddles allowed her to weave the threads easily as she simply moved forward one heddle for the first row and moved the other heddle forward for the next row.

The horizontal rows are called the weft.

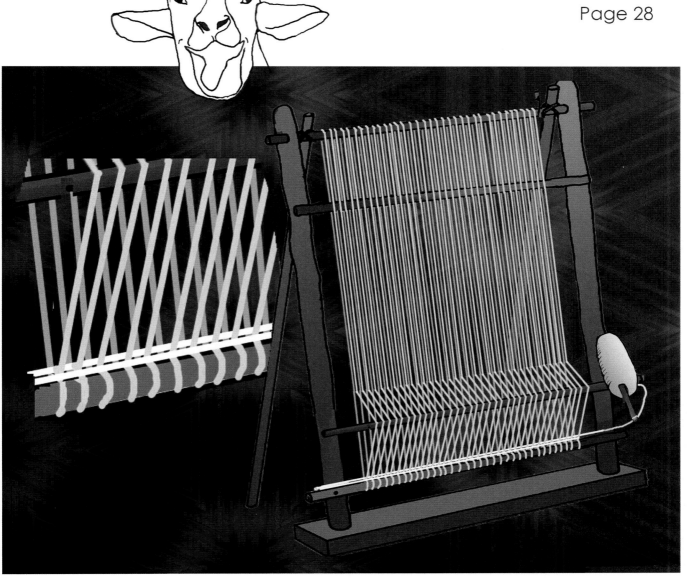

In order to create the wonderful colored pattern that would become the finished rug, each square in the cartoon had to be duplicated by a "knot" of colored wool on the loom.

These "knots" were actually loops through two adjacent warp threads on the loom.

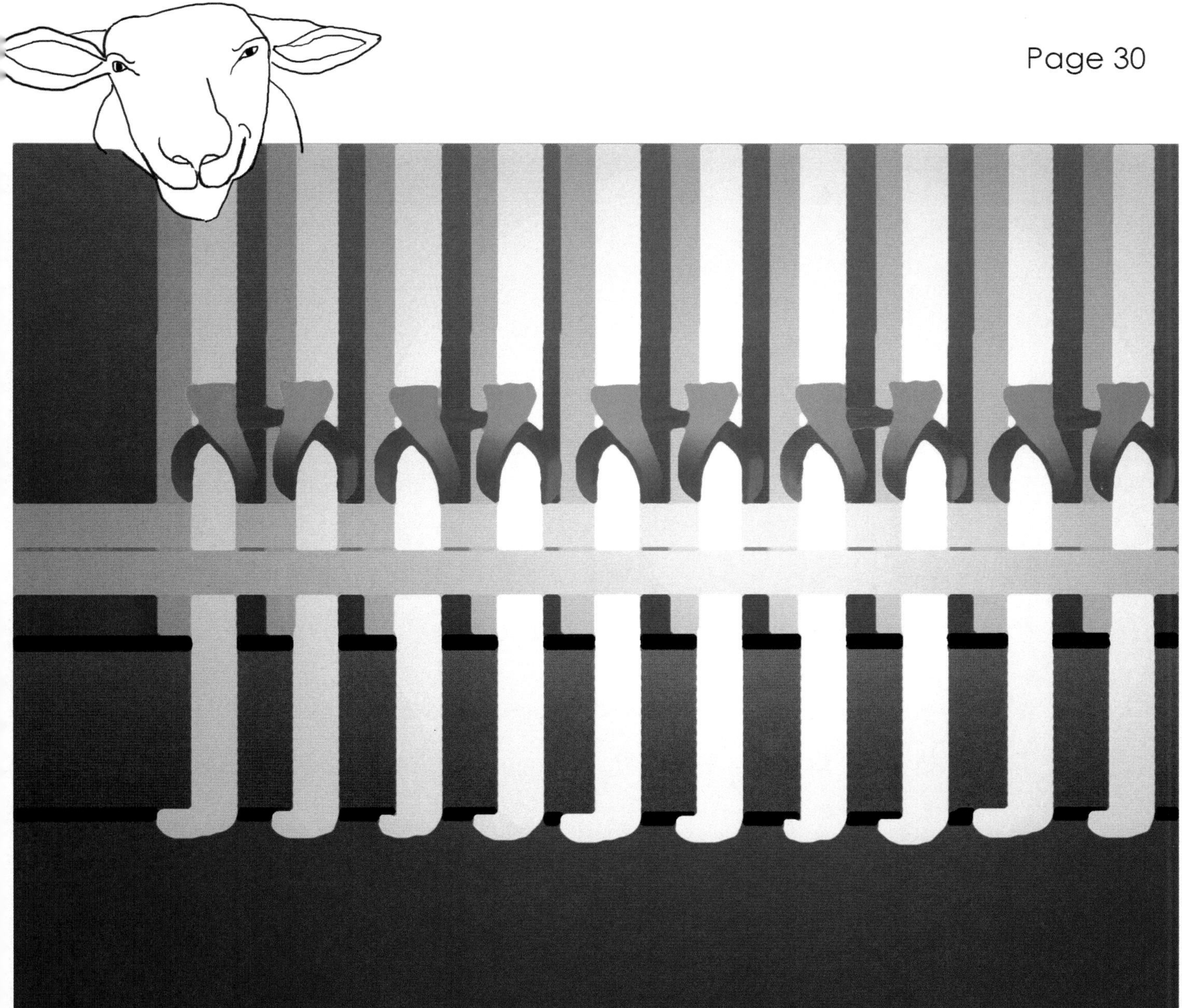

Talya was now old enough to work on the rug. Carefully following the cartoon, she tied knots. She added two weft threads after each row of knots and tamped them down tight.

Many months passed and the rug began to take shape.

Many, many small knots had to be
carefully wrapped and tamped down
before I became the magnificent rug
I am today.
(Pardon my bragging please)

During this time Talya grew into
a beautiful young woman and
fell in love with none other than
the young man who sheared me
so many years before.

The two lovers married and Talya presented me to her new husband.

Unfortunately this joy did not last too long as there was tribal warfare in the villages near where the happy couple lived, and Talya's husband was called to fight. He did not want to fight his neighbors or leave his new bride. They were in despair about this turn of events when a man came into their village looking for rugs. He was the curator from a museum in the United States.

Talya saw an answer to their troubles and proudly showed me to this learned man. He was extremely impressed with my beauty and the careful workmanship that went into my creation.

Talya told the Museum curator that she would only part with me if she and her husband could accompany me on the ship to America.

The curator reluctantly agreed to the huge expense of their passage.

So off they all went on camels to the nearest port where they set sail for America.

The trip was very long and rocky and Talya and her new husband thought they might never see land again, but I was rolled up in a corner of the curator's cabin, nice and dry, and I rather enjoyed the experience.

Once we arrived in America I was taken to a large museum in a big city where I was rolled out to great fanfare in the magnificent halls of a marvelous place with treasures from all over the world.

And here I still hang admired by all who pass by.

Talya's great grandchildren come to visit sometimes. To tell the truth, I don't think they believe that she created me so long ago and so far away, but it makes me happy to see them as I know they would not be here without me.

Nancy Clearwater Herman is a fiber artist, painter, Illustrator and videographer. She has work in over 100 private and public collections, including the Philadelphia Museum of Art, The Museum of the State of Pennsylvania, the Brevard Museum In Florida and the San Jose Museum of Quilts and Textiles.

She has authored and illustrated several books. If C IS RED, published by Blurb Books, which details her method of translating music to color, OLIVE AND STICKY BEAR, AND JOE AND THE ADOBIANS, both children's books, and POSTCARDS FROM MERION and POSTCARDS FROM BROOKLYN, books that include paintings and musings from her blog, Postcards From Merion. These were all published by Createspace and are available there and at AMAZON.com.

Aram Jerrehian is a retired oriental rug dealer and the author of ORIENTAL RUG PRIMER, Philadelphia, Running Press, 1980. He conducted courses in the Department of General Studies at the University of Pennsylvania, was a senior member of the American Society of Appraisers and co-founder of the Oriental Rug Retailers of America.

Made in the USA
Middletown, DE
08 May 2021